How to do Perfect Murder –
The Art of Killing

Prologue

It is matter of intense comedy –how clowns are killed –especially around the middle of October. These clowns should be killed around middle October because if they ask for drinks –either hot or cold –you would not run out of options.

A glass of Vodka would be sufficient and you would neither need a refrigerator or heater.

Disclaimer: This is a work of fiction to tickle your funny bone. This book has a vodka label: "Do not try this at home" –because you might land up in the wrong side of law.

Chapters

Chapter One: The Pain

Murder in professional style is the USP of Professional Killers. If the killers had attended Harvard or Indian Institute of Management Ahmedabad –then on the murder day they might have worn Armani Suit, Reebok Shoes, and Rayban

Glasses and have cremated the dead body in Audi A6.

The guns would have been gold-plated Remington and there might have been six fake bullets in the pack of 12.

People commit murder —not because of enmity — but because the victim had crossed limits in irritating the perpetrator. Murder is always the last option —an end to the means —a method of madness.

The killers always wanted their victim to surrender, but the stubborn attitude of victim force the killer to get him/her out of the way.

Everyone have weak areas —and instead of working in weak areas —if somebody starts weakening it further —then the murder happens.

The victims have the weakest phase of their lives just before the Murder, yet they profess that they are in their strongest position. Surrender is always the best option, and if the victim had surrendered, he might not have been murdered.

Now in typical management style let us work on prime reasons —why a person is selected for murder. The pain areas are:

1. A person who is not returning your money
2. A wife or husband who is cheating on you
3. A family member who is hindrance to your love
4. A person who is constantly irritating you
5. A person who is constantly blackmailing you
6. A person from whom you want to seek revenge
7. A person who is constantly hurting your ideals
8. A person who is always making empty promises
9. A girl who gets you sexcited and leaves you high and dry
10. An Employer —who fired you from job —and your worst days started from there.

In case of (1), (2), (6), (7), (8), (9), and (10) —the things can be easily sorted out by sitting across the table. But in case (4), (5), Murder is the only option.

In case (3) —just keep on having sex with your partner and go for court marriage or marry with Islamic Rituals.

Chapter 2: SWOT Analysis

Before getting into details of murders, let us get into the Psychology of Murder. This act is committed mostly as marketing tool. It will enhance your image as brand, send fear down your opponents and make a perfect bonding with your team for further missions.

Let us talk about Murder as a major marketing tool and discuss it as 4P's of marketing.

- Product —Here the Product is your victim
- Price —The Price is the credibility you earn after the act
- Promotion —The Promotion is the brand recognition your team earns

- Place —The Place is the location where you dispose the body.

I well remember about a Member of Parliament – Pappu Yadav –who became a brand instantly after the murder of Ajit Sarkar –and amassed huge wealth after the act. He won elections, was feared through-out the Bihar and got connected with almost all powerful people of North and East India.

He was in Jail for few days, but later discharged by CBI court.

If a murder can bring such fame, recognition, power, money and authority –then why do not go for it. Treat it as business opportunity.

Murder is like selling a product. You have to first research about product and develop a solid product.

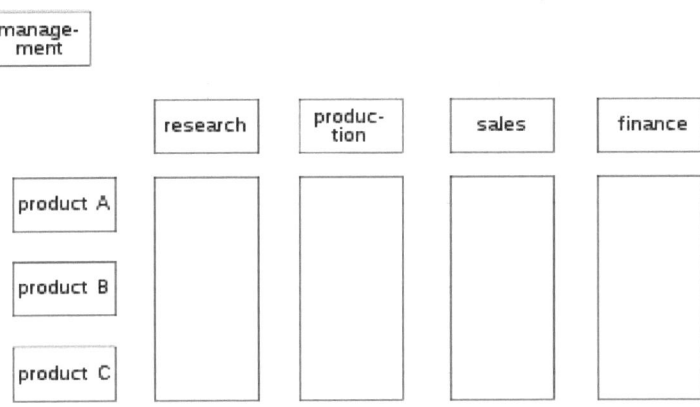

By doing research you develop many prototype of product, do beta run, test the product on a small sample, get the feedback from target consumers and then launch the product in a limited market.

(By speaking foolishly –I am talking about the team of hired killers)

Then not engaging a large amount of capital, your product goes to production stage. You are always scared that product might fail and your money would be wasted. (Clownishly you are scared that your henchmen would be caught by Police and you would have to arrange their bail).

Then there comes sales. You have to make a team of buffoons —who would market your product. (It is like arranging weapons in National Capital Region, Gujarat or UP).

If you are successful until this stage, then comes the real problem —you have to scale your operation. You have to arrange financiers like Infosys, TCS. Reliance, Adani and Microsoft to go for mass production. (In normal murders, a supari of small amount is given initially, and when killers start moving towards target in 3 teams, you have to pay huge amount to their family members —the risks for killers are injury, jail, death or life-imprisonment).

Now let us discuss the Strength, Weakness, Opportunity and Threat (SWOT) analysis of the murder plan.

A typical table would look like:

	Strength	Weakness	Opportunity	Threat
1	Ready to Die	No Money	Fame	Jail Sentence
2	Motivated	Less Money	Money	Expenditure
3	Good Team	Bragging	Power	Distrust
4	Good Network	Getting Soft on Target	Position	Ignominy
5	Alibi	Falling Ill	Weak Enemies	Disease
6	Good Wives	Pardoning Victim	Love and Admiration of Wives	Being Reborn in Family

Now draw a list of your enemies and make your priority from bottom to top. Start hitting from bottom until you reach the top. My list is:

1. Anonymous
2. Prachi
3. Mandana
4. First Husband
5. Shambhavi
6. Deepika
7. Priyanka
8. Neha Sharma (Aryasamaj)
9. Mamta
10. Shivani
11. Neha Don
12. Melanie
13. Neha Lawanda
14. Aishwarya Don
15. Katrina
16. Urvashi (Rourkela)

17. Sonia
18. Nora
19. Diana
20. Nyusha
21. Vannessa
22. Babul
23. Anonymous
24. Anonymous

A top down approach would hurt you, but bottom up approach will give you least resistance.

Chapter 3: Cornering the Victim

Murder is like Nirvana. It releases immense amount of Negative energy from your brain and fills you with positivity. The pain inflicted to you by your enemy should be severely inflicted back to them. While murdering you should match words to words; phrase to phrase; text to text. You should hurt him so badly during the act that so that his rebirth should either be paralytic or as a mental patient –

very weak, very meek –and with tons of positive attitude.

But some souls are like snake video game of Casio. By eating victims, they grow mightier and mightier – to offend more, to spread filth, to die more gory death.

Everyone has same flesh and bone. The Intel Chip of body is the soul. A soul is good or bad –not the body. So according to our scriptures, after death, a body is reformed and worst form of torture is unleashed on evil people.

In my experience in jail –I found that most of the people who are murdered are conspirators –who conspire to ruin the life of somebody through chain of conspiracies. The brave people like Bhagat Singh, Rajguru, Sukhdev, Chandrasekhar Azad, Pappu Yadav and Syed Sahabuddin take direct action without conspiracy.

Obviously a plan is needed but is not called conspiracy. There is major difference between plan and conspiracy. A conspiracy –like proxy war –is to torture your enemy, but a plan is to eliminate the disturbing and malicious element forever –for the general good of society.

For example 9/11 and 26/11 were conspiracy, but US action in Tora-Bora and Surgical strike across LOC was plan.

Now let me show some insight into BitCoin of Universe. Narad Muni is the founder of BitCoin. Let us say it as FitCoin. He is very garrulous and talkative. He does not have any job –and to constantly entertain his vast audience –he says something. He just says something out of air just for fun and then something happens somewhere, then fearing that it will harm the Demons –they run to make sure that this does not happen –the Gods run to make it happen. The conflict between Gods and Demon arise.

To ensure the victory of Gods –Lord Ganesh makes the plan; Lord Vishnu drafts the plan and Lord Shiva's army implement the plan.

So this is happening all the time in Universe. Most often the sayings of Narada Muni are influenced by childish mistakes of Lord Vishnu. If Narada Muni kept his mouth shut then there would have been no trouble in Universe. And Lord Vishnu is very innocent –whatever he does innocently is due to suffering he undergoes while running the Universe.

**

If there have been no Lord Vishnu –the world would have been run by demons. He is most innocent and loving of all Gods. He loves everybody and pardons everybody. But seeing his benevolence the demons trick him into defeat. Then comes Kartikeya –he is tough task master and best at his ruthlessness. He never lost any war in his life. His entry in the battlefield is so severe that many demons die with heart-attack only by hearing his name.

**

Now let me throw some insight into the army of gods. They are by nature subtle and weak. In war they are always dominated by demons –then come the magic recipe like spinach of Popeye and Goggles of "May I come in Madam". They drink a cup of tea and become very strong. Kartikeya always sits on the fringe of battle-field and enjoy divine music. Whenever Gods have to kill a big warrior they call him –he slays the warrior and again exit battlefield to enjoy music.

**

According to #gandu #puran –the slam book of Gods –the most innocent creature of universe is #snake. Be like snake in real life –stay away from all controversies –but someone hurts you –then devastate him.

**

Now coming to Kashmir controversy, the problem could have been solved in 1947 itself –either it had been part of India or Pakistan. Solution should have been decided by International consensus and had been strictly implanted. There had not been three wars –and so much bloodshed. The fault was in vision of Sardar Vallabh Bhai Patel. He had lack of vision. He was iron man within India –but could not analyze –where trouble lied. A decisive war in 1947 could have laid everything to rest.

Similarly there are assholes in your life. They keep you disturbing every time. You pardon them every time and they create trouble of increased intensity. Killing is never the best option. You should try to load as many #courtcases and #policecases as possible to nail them forever.

**

Evil in society crops up mostly by virtue of good people. If offenders are punished in the nascent stage of their nuisance then there have been no evil in the society.

**

As far I am concerned I am Innocent. Whatever crimes I committed was due to my insecurity. My husband did land related scams only to lead a lavish and luxurious lifestyle –not with intention of hurting others. I am not a bitch; I am Tommy –that is because I wear Tommy Hilfiger.

**

The men with good intentions have a serious calm on their face –that makes their opponent terrified. Because their opponents know –when butcher goes on roll –there would be death, destruction and blood everywhere.

**

Now let us talk about man-woman relationship. There is one simple rule for ideal wife –obey your husband. All problems crop up in man-woman relationship because the wife or girl does not obey her husband or boyfriend. The life of such girls is full of struggles, and such relationships end in break-up or divorce.

Patient guys tolerate such relationship by staying away from their wives. Impatient guys seek emotional support and motivation from other girls.

**

Please do not escalate disturbed relationships to a point, where a girl or guy has no option other than getting rid of their spouse. Man woman relationship is best when the girl is exactly opposite of guy. An aggressive girl can never stay with aggressive guy. A meek guy can never stay with meek girl.

**

An example of failed relationship from movie industry is Brad-Pitt and Angelina Jolie. Their life was reduced to mess/hour.

**

My father who is Shirdi Sai Baba reborn is a movie buff. He watches TV all day long. While watching TV he said a dialogue -"The mission of my life is to establish order –one who offends me, either surrender or die". This became motto of my life after divine enlightment. I got divine enlightment after brutal mental torture between 22 December 2012 and 11 January 2013.

**

I have always thought for others, once my basic necessities were met. I am a Fedayeen or mercenary –and for that reason I did not spare my father –when he started treading on wrong path.

**

The path of God is always filled with tremendous resistance. But the benefit is that the most powerful force of God is always supportive.

**

Let me quote an incident when I was in hospital. I always feared that my relatives will die when they came to meet me because of dangerous roads. One day in fear I faked chest pain. The doctor recommended me ECG –and that simple test paved my way for miraculous escape from that extremely torturous hospital.

In that hospital I had only two thoughts 24x7 – murder or suicide; murder or suicide; murder or suicide.

**

My life got organized after escape from that hospital. I started acquiring perfection after that torture. The odds were always stacked against me, but like a Fedayeen –I started to live with bare minimum necessities. I started building lethal teams and multiple level of hierarchy in my defense mechanism so that before reaching me my enemies are terminated by my loyalists.

I began to strategize. I never tried too hard to achieve anything. I always adhered to solutions that really worked. I had very deep and emotional feelings for people who cared about me –with the simple thought that love is reciprocal.

I started taking my enemies by surprise. I started weaving a network around my enemies in such a manner that they are hit by same people who they used to attack me.

But the real pain of my life still remained the same – a person very close to me in my family.

**

The best strategy which I developed to attack my enemy is to launch attacks on them –months before the final showdown. I shared my all my plans with my trusted lieutenants –fearing that if my plan is leaked by a traitor, then my men will launch instant attacks to nullify any negative effect on me.

**

Two of my aides Jaikaal –from Preacher and crow – from Venus Williams, were given supernatural powers to unleash mass onslaught –if a formidable army of opponents start approaching me or my family members. Flirt Kimi – a die-hard maniac and thousand times more offensive than any living mortal was entrusted to create havoc through cyclones, floods and earthquakes.

The team of waaris –trained by Shiva Guru Utthapa himself were trained to carry surgical strikes –like heart-attack, kidney and liver failure or instant paralysis.

**

My kid Damn from Deepak –could make strongest hearted men, women or eunuch –mental patient within minutes. My kid Panic –from Prem could dishearten –the strongest of army within minutes and they will start leaving from the battlefield. My kid Nail from –Ahant could confuse the enemies to such an extent that they start killing their own men and women. My kid Dum from Dhoopnath Singh could instill so much zeal in my men that even from the weakest position in battlefield –they can rout any number and configuration of enemies.

**

These kids are too much present and will meet my spouse very soon. (I am right now in Hell –writing this book, and ordering good food for new and dear visitors).

**

Chapter 4: Alibi

I am Fidayeen, and mass murderer –but I always have excuses when law catches with me. I am busy with my husband doing good work whenever there is cop raid at my Lutyens house:

1. With Deepak –Managing Mental Hospitals
2. With Preacher –Managing world-wide catering
3. With Priyank –Managing Global Schools

4. With Madhur Karim –Managing Chain of Religious Institutions
5. With Ahan Samrat –Managing Orphanages and Old age Asha.
6. With Lesbian girlfriend Nayi Asha – Power Corp of World
7. With Nehal Dhupari – Managing world-wide textiles
8. With Milane Arya – Funding and Micro Funding
9. With Venus Williams –The world of sports.

I am either in Jail or with these guys –whenever a crime happens. Though I am a known criminal, the law avoids me. I fear my foes might copy my strategy and launch counter-attack on me, so I am writing this book to spread knowledge internally to my team mates.

Chapter 5: Execution

Once you have team, guns, finances and alibi in place, then move to target in multiple teams. Keep multiple backups to encounter any resistance. Kill the target(s) and go underground. Behave as if nothing has happened. Party, Dance and Enjoy. Concentrate on creative pursuits.

**

End of Fuck! (Sorry –end of book!)

The perfect plan is executed with minimal effort and least resistance –Lord Karti Gosh (Religious Head – RPM, Vasant Vihar, Delhi)

www.ingramcontent.com/pod-product-compliance
Lightning Source LLC
Chambersburg PA
CBHW041620180526
45159CB00002BC/951